When someone a
God allow suffer
suggests three th

loving and caring—
that is why some
think it strange that
God allows suffering.

Second, that He
has the power to stop suffering—
otherwise the word 'allow' would mean nothing.

Third, that He will finally eliminate suffering—logic says
that if there is a God who is eternal and good, He will ban
suffering from Heaven.

The Bible agrees with each of these three suggestions! God
is loving and caring; He is in control; and He is eternal
and will finally eliminate
suffering. He will
keep precisely to His
timetable to deal with
and banish it. Let's look
at these suggestions one
by one.

3

1. God loves and cares

The Bible teaches that God is a God of love; in fact He *is* love!

The greatest love between man and woman is as nothing compared with God's love for us.

The best of human love can be spoiled and soiled by selfishness. It sometimes suffers with our mood swings. It rarely attaches to unlovely people.

Compare this with God's love. It is faithful, pure, selfless and constant. It never changes or evaporates. God even loves those who reject and ignore Him and hurt others by their wrongdoing.

Does God's allowing suffering, or even causing it, mean that His love has evaporated?

Certainly not! God loved us so much that He gave His Son, the Lord Jesus Christ, to come to Earth to die on the cross for us. That was despite, and because of, man's sinful rebellion against Him.

On the cross He suffered the judgement we deserve for our sins. He rose again, and lives today. In His amazing love, God gives eternal life to those who personally trust in Christ.

When Christ comes to live in the heart of someone who turns from wrongdoing to Him, God fills that person with His love and changes him or her from within.

Chapter 3 verse 16 of John's Gospel (quoted below) declares that God's love to us, shown in history, becomes real and effective for anyone who trusts in, or believes in, the Lord Jesus Christ:

**FOR
GOD SO LOVED THE WORLD THAT HE GAVE HIS
ONLY BEGOTTEN
SON, THAT WHOEVER BELIEVES IN HIM SHOULD NOT
PERISH BUT HAVE
EVERLASTING
LIFE.'**

Note: **G O S P E L** = 'good news'

2. God is all-powerful

God has limitless power as sovereign Creator. He can do anything consistent with His will and wisdom.

Think of the vastness of immeasurable space, the dazzling brightness and searing heat of the sun, the magnificence of an electric storm, the majestic power of an angry sea, or the crashing splendour of Niagara or Victoria Falls.

The elephant's strength, the whale's size, the cheetah's speed, the eagle's soaring ascents and breathtaking dives—all reflect their Creator's mighty strength and design.

Jesus worked mighty miracles, signs showing that Jesus was God come in the flesh as man.

The sick, the blind, the deaf, the mute and the lame were healed by Him. He raised the dead to life. He conquered His own tomb! He rose from the dead and ascended into Heaven. He is Lord!

History also testifies that God powerfully changes lives. The abolition of slave trading, care of forsaken orphans, relief for overworked and bullied women and children, hope for hopeless drunkards, life-changing love for prisoners—all this and a lot more has come through people whose lives were changed by Jesus Christ.

Consider the following people as examples: the once-blaspheming slave trader, John Newton; the former arrogant sceptic, Dr Barnardo; the tireless politician, William Wilberforce; the outcast's champion, General Booth; the prison reformer, Elizabeth Fry. Each one was mightily transformed by God's saving power.

Anyone trusting in Jesus Christ today, however bad and broken his or her life may be, still experiences God's lifechanging power.

Because God is almighty, He can stop or relieve suffering at any time. Thus all suffering is *allowed* by God.

The Bible shows that for special, justified reasons God sometimes even causes it. His eternal judgement on those who refuse to turn from sin to Christ for forgiveness is the worst of all suffering.

3. God will finally eliminate suffering

Let's look at the start of the world and then at its finish.

The Bible teaches that no suffering existed on Planet Earth at the start. Everything that God created was *very good*. In fact, it reflected its perfect Creator.

The Bible also makes it clear that there will be no suffering finally.

We shall see on the following page that something went wrong in-between.

The glorious and powerful return to this world of the Lord Jesus Christ will usher in events leading to the creation of a new Heaven and a new Earth. Perfection will be restored there and then.

First, He will remove this current creation, with its sin and suffering, like a dirty tablecloth.

Suffering originated from man's sin and disobedience that caused God to curse the Earth.

But God's Word says that both sin and suffering have a 'shelf life'. One day, they will be no more in Heaven for those who have trusted in Christ.

It is hard for us to grasp that truth in our wicked and hurting world. We are too involved in wrong and suffering to think objectively.

But, finally, sin will be excluded from God's new Heaven and Earth. With sin banished, all resulting suffering, pain and sadness will disappear. God will eliminate it all—completely, utterly and fully.

At that time, God will wipe away every tear from each eye. Death will be no more. Sorrow and crying will be kept out. No one will ever suffer pain then. Everything will be changed.

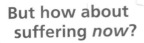

But how about suffering *now*?

Suffering certainly does exist *now*! So the question *How can God allow suffering?* is relevant. After all, we all live in a world of great suffering.

Why do we suffer *now*?

Suffering often comes from three main sources: from natural causes; from other people; and from me.

Our newspapers and TV reports are full of natural calamities, wars and strife, and the harm and hurt caused by the wickedness and selfishness of individuals.

For some, it seems hardest to accept the suffering that results from the malfunction of fallen and cursed nature, be it by disease or catastrophe. It seems to them that the only person left to blame—if He exists at all—is God!

Also, we all suffer because of others, and all cause suffering to others. We even cause some suffering to ourselves.

The suffering that I cause to others by my wrongdoing may not reach the media headlines, but I know it is a fact. So does God!

10

Some suffering results from natural causes

Suffering through natural causes hits everyone. Their individual guilt or innocence is irrelevant.

This is as true of measles, influenza, cancer and heart disease as it is of earthquakes, tsunamis, storms, floods, volcanic eruptions, famines and droughts. Illnesses, accidents, calamities and death affect us all.

All this suffering results from being part of a fallen world. God cursed the Earth after man sinned against Him. Nature and mankind have been living with the consequences of that sin and punishment ever since.

To stop this suffering, God would need to renew the whole world. As we have seen, He will do this at the right time— but not yet.

2. Some suffering is caused by other people

Millions of people suffer at the hands of others. That is so internationally, nationally, locally, in the family, and individually.

War, terrorism, famine, Aids, violence, dishonesty, greed, lust, robbery, immorality, cruelty, and selfishness—all these have claimed millions of victims worldwide. They all result from 'man's inhumanity to man'.

Some calamities with a natural element have been caused or worsened by man's sinfulness. Famine, for example, often occurs where there is war. Profiteering often stops donated food reaching victims.

In any case, there is enough food in the world to feed everyone—yet half the world starves while the other half eats too much and has to diet for health reasons.

Imagine how different TV news and our newspapers would be if men and women did not cheat, hurt, abuse, fight and kill one another!

Imagine the change in newscasts and headlines if a genuine love for one another motivated all people to help others in need and never to harm anyone!

But the sad truth is that selfishness reigns. In disobeying God, people do not love their neighbours as themselves. On the contrary, they often harm others wilfully or by neglect. This causes suffering.

To stop this suffering caused by others, God would need to judge and remove all offenders from everywhere around the globe. He will do this— but not yet. He has His timetable and He will keep it.

But see pages 14 and 15, overleaf. Remember that we all have made other people suffer through our selfishness and sins. Unless we turn from our sins to Christ for forgiveness we also will suffer God's punishment for our sins eternally.

3. Some suffering is caused by me

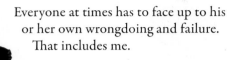

Everyone at times has to face up to his or her own wrongdoing and failure. That includes me.

It is so easy to see wrong in others and not to own up to my own guilt. But I, too, have to admit that I also rebel against God and His standards. That often means I treat others badly as a result.

That is why I sometimes cheat and lie. I find it easy to be greedy, cruel and immoral in thought, word or deed.

Even if I do not physically assault someone, I often harbour an aggressive and mean spirit within. Lust and hate are sometimes in my heart. At times, only circumstances or fear stops me acting badly. In my heart I am guilty— and often in my actions and words also.

I must own up to it: I am basically selfish. Because I offend God and hurt and upset others by my sins, I, too, am guilty of causing suffering. It is no defence to say that others offend, too.

Some suffering I cause to others is direct and intentional—that is when I do something obviously wrong.

I am also guilty of not seeking to help or alleviate others' suffering. Why? Because I am too selfish to put myself out to help people in need. That is suffering caused by my omissions or neglect.

Either way, my actions or omissions have a bad effect on others. Others suffer because of me.

To stop this suffering caused by me, God would need to deal with me personally. You will see later in this booklet how He will do this in one of two ways.

Could not God step in to stop all suffering immediately?

The *real* question which many ask is not just, *How can a God of love allow suffering?* People also want to know *Why doesn't God stop the suffering **now**?* If God allows or causes suffering, surely He can stop it immediately?

Would it not be better for everyone if God intervened *now* to remove all suffering?

Some may say that it is OK to philosophize about what may happen in the future, but, right now, people are dying in famines and wars. As you read this there are new victims of murder, rape, child abuse, violence, dishonesty and unfaithfulness.

So they ask the question, *Why not stop all this right now?* Interestingly, that same question is asked in the Bible.

To stop that suffering now and to remain consistent, God would need *now* to remove from the world *all* suffering—not just the suffering which we hear about or hate most.

Can you visualize a world with no illnesses, accidents, tsunamis, famines, wars, terrorism, crime, violence, dishonesty, unfaithfulness, lust, or cruelty in words or deeds? It would be a perfect world!

It would mean removing the causes of suffering. There would be no Hitlers, terrorists, murderers, rapists, paedophiles, adulterers, thieves, cheats or liars. But wait a minute! Follow this through. Nothing would be allowed to remain that would defile or offend. God would need to remove *every single offender*. That must include *me and you*.

Just like all other offenders, we, too, deserve God's judgement for our many sins. There would be no exceptions or favouritism—all must come under God's eternal judgement, which is the final fulfilment of His curse on sin.

At the right time, God will put suffering right and deal as Judge with all wrongs and with all wrongdoers who cause suffering. But He delays now to give each of us time to turn *from* all our wrongdoings *to* Him for forgiveness.

If He judged everyone right now, it would be too late for some to come to Christ for forgiveness. That would include you, if you have not yet come to Christ.

Why don't we suffer more than we do?

Neither you nor I deserve to live in a perfect world. We are not perfect ourselves.

Often, we accept God's enormous blessings without gratitude, as if we deserved them. Yet we are very quick to grumble and groan when we suffer, as if we did not deserve it.

Yet we have added to a hurting world by our sins—against God and against others. In small or big ways, we have damaged others' lives, reputations or peace of mind by selfishness and doing wrong.

Perhaps the question we ought to ask, therefore, is, *Why do we not suffer more than we do?* If our only defence against suffering was our innocence, none of us could ever have any relief from it. We are guilty! Can we seriously argue with that?

But, mercifully, God has not written us off. Although the time will come when He will judge sinners, His arms of mercy are still open to us now. No one knows when that opportunity will close.

We have seen that, if God stepped in *immediately* to put suffering right and to punish wrongdoers, it would then be too late to turn to Christ as Saviour for forgiveness. The opportunity for some—perhaps even you—to be saved would have gone for ever. God's judgement and eternal punishment would be unavoidable.

That is why God commands everyone everywhere to repent and trust Him *now*, while there is still time.

To repent means to be so sorry for your sins and guilt that you admit them with shame and turn from them to God, asking for His mercy and forgiveness. You must do a U-turn.

U-turn

If you have not yet come to Jesus Christ, you need *urgently* to ask Him to help you make that U-turn from sin, to forgive you, and to become your Saviour.

To delay repenting and coming to Christ is worse than refusing to leave a building after a police warning that a bomb will explode soon. A bomb warning can be false, and you may survive an explosion. But God's warning to repent and trust Him is genuine: the consequences of not doing so are eternal.

How can anyone escape who ignores God's warning?

Four important reminders

The question *How can God allow suffering?* should remind us of four important things:

1. We are weak and just passing through this world.

Life is short. It is like a vapour. Suffering reminds us how weak we are and that our lives here are temporary.

One man may be in his prime: strong, intelligent, well qualified, rich, gifted and self-sufficient. He may strut around like a peacock.

But he does not know how long or happy his life will be. See him if a tsunami strikes, or as a victim of a terrorist bomb or car crash, or after the ravages of cancer, or even as he grows weaker in old age.

We are in a queue moving through life and our turn to go will come. Sometimes we jump the queue unexpectedly. One thing is sure: one day each of us will die.

2. *Suffering is often God's megaphone or alarm clock.*

Our very vulnerability in suffering can make us seek God and listen for His voice. Someone once said that God whispers to us through our blessings, speaks to us through our hardships and shouts at us through our sufferings. That is one reason why He allows or causes them.

God gets our attention through our sufferings. Sadly, when all seems well, we can easily ignore God. Suffering can be His megaphone to speak to us, or his alarm clock to wake us up.

Without a really deep sense of need of God, some people would never seek Him or call on Him.

Strangely, the things we want to avoid, but cannot—such as illness, injury, weakness, failure, loss, disappointment, others' unfaithfulness or opposition, bereavement or facing our own deaths—can become agents of blessing helping us to seek God. They can become that megaphone or alarm clock.

3. Jesus Christ has suffered for us.

God the Father knows what it feels like to see His one and only Son, the Lord Jesus Christ, be cruelly treated by men to the point of death. Jesus personally suffered shame, pain and separation on the cross. Here was the One who was, at the same time, perfectly God and perfectly man—our *Immanuel, God with us*—dying for us.

Yet He had never sinned. He never deserved to suffer. He was completely sinless and righteous. He willingly went to the cross to suffer and die for us. He was cursed for us when He bore our sins and their judgement. Our hell fell on Him.

The Bible teaches that Jesus *suffered ... the just for the unjust, [to] bring us to God*, when *He bore our sins in His own body* on the cross for us. He was *stricken, smitten by God, and afflicted* when He willingly took God's punishment for our sins there.

He rose from the dead and lives today. Jesus Christ came on a rescue mission *to seek and to save that which*

was lost. He saves from sin and Hell all who call upon Him to pardon and save them. He is our only lifeboat in the stormy sea of wrongdoing, guilt and judgement. Without Him, we are lost.

Those who turn their backs on their sins and ask Jesus to enter their lives to save them will enjoy a perfect eternity with Him. It will be entirely free of pain and suffering, and unsurpassable in its peace, joy and glory for evermore.

Those who know Christ will still suffer in this life. Much suffering is common to Christians and to non-Christians as human beings. But sometimes, Christians suffer simply because they follow Christ in a hostile world. Persecution, isolation, discrimination, imprisonment, victimization, deprivation and death are commonplace for some 21st-century Christians.

But those who know Jesus Christ personally experience his presence, peace and help, whatever their sufferings.

They will share an eternity of suffering-free bliss with their Saviour, which He promises all who receive Him by faith.

23

4. God's longsuffering in not intervening gives you time to get right with Him.

God now delays before fulfilling His promise to put everything right finally.

The Lord Jesus Christ will return to judge sin and renew everything.

But He is longsuffering towards us. He wants no one to perish. That is why He commands all people to repent. Some will repent and be forgiven. Some will not.

For those who refuse to repent, Christ's second coming will come as frighteningly sudden and unexpected as a burglar in the night.

Then everything in our Heaven and Earth will be destroyed—and the opportunity for sinners to trust Christ as Saviour will have gone for ever. It will be too late to come to know Jesus as Lord and Saviour.

When God brings in His perfect and new Heaven and Earth, and the everlasting reign of righteousness, there will be no more suffering. Righteousness, peace and joy will rule!

Those who know Jesus will benefit there for ever from God's mercy and grace.

But for now, God delays His inevitable judgement and future timetable to allow guilty sinners time to repent and trust Him now.

Who knows when the midnight hour might strike? We must be ready. Nothing is more important than where we spend eternity. Our only two options are to *repent* or to *perish*. If we repent, we will never perish eternally. Any who perish eternally will not have repented and trusted Jesus Christ.

If you have not already done so, are you willing to repent and turn to Christ to forgive you now?

A word about prayer

As we have seen, even if you turn to Christ, you will face some suffering in life sometime. But in it you can know God's peace, presence, help, strength and comfort. His grace is sufficient for all your needs.

When a real Christian suffers, he or she should commit it to God by praying, and keep trusting Him. The Bible gives an account of a man called Job. He suffered terribly in different ways. In the worst of it, he said of God, *Though He slay me, yet will I trust Him*. He never knew why he suffered, but he hung on to God by faith. This is hard, but God still blesses those who trust Him like that today.

And no matter what you suffer on Earth, remember that your personal faith in Christ guarantees you to be with Him in Heaven.

Let me make it clear: if you receive Christ you will avoid the Hell you deserve to suffer and receive God's undeserved gift of eternal life.

It is always good to pray to God. Some prayers are long. But a short prayer from the heart can be the key into God's presence. God looks at your heart.

Some helpful prayers from the Bible

Below are some short prayers from the Bible. Why not make them your own?

Just repeating words like a parrot is not prayer at all. But if you mean the words in your heart and ask Jesus Christ to take over in your life as your Lord and Saviour, God hears your prayer.

God will always answer your prayer if you sincerely confess your sins to Him, turn from them and put all your confidence in the Lord Jesus Christ as your Saviour.

'LORD, I BELIEVE; HELP MY UNBELIEF'
Mark 9:24

'LORD, REMEMBER ME'
Luke 23:42

'HELP, LORD'
Psalm 12:1

'CREATE IN ME A CLEAN HEART, O GOD'
Psalm 51:10

'GOD, BE MERCIFUL TO ME A SINNER'
Luke 18:13

'LORD, SAVE ME!'
Matthew 14:30

Isaiah 52:13–53:12

Behold, My Servant shall
deal prudently;
He shall be exalted and
extolled and be
very high.
Just as many were
astonished at you,
So His visage was marred
more than any man,
And His form more than
the sons of men ...

Who has believed our
report?
And to whom has the arm
of the Lord been
revealed?
For He shall grow up
before Him as a tender
plant,
And as a root out of dry
ground.
He has no form or
comeliness;
And when we see Him,

There is no beauty that we
should desire Him.
He is despised and rejected
by men,
A Man of sorrows and
acquainted with grief.
And we hid, as it were,
our faces from Him;
He was despised, and we
did not esteem Him.
Surely He has borne our
griefs
And carried our sorrows;
Yet we esteemed Him
stricken,
Smitten by God, and
afflicted.
But He was wounded for
our transgressions,
He was bruised for our
iniquities;
The chastisement for our
peace was upon Him,
And by His stripes we are
healed.
All we like sheep have gone
astray;

We have turned, every one,
  to his own way;
And the Lord has laid on
  Him the iniquity of
  us all.
He was oppressed and He
  was afflicted,
Yet He opened not His
  mouth;
He was led as a lamb to the
  slaughter,
And as a sheep before its
  shearers is silent,
So He opened not His
  mouth ...

For the transgressions of
  My people He was
  stricken.
And they made His grave
  with the wicked—
But with the rich at His
  death,
Because He had done no
  violence,
Nor was any deceit in His
  mouth.
Yet it pleased the Lord to
  bruise Him;
He has put Him to grief.
When You make His soul
  an offering for sin,
He shall see His seed, He
  shall prolong His days,
And the pleasure of the
  Lord shall prosper in
  His hand.
He shall see the labour of
  His soul, and be satisfied.
By His knowledge My
  righteous Servant shall
  justify many,
For He shall bear their
  iniquities.
Therefore I will divide
  Him a portion with the
  great ...

Because He poured out
  His soul unto death,
And He was numbered
  with the transgressors,
And He bore the sin of
  many,
And made intercession for
  the transgressors.

Please look up the Bible references given below, which apply to the pages shown.

This booklet reflects the teaching of the Bible, God's Word. (As a guide, Romans 8:38–39 is the book of Romans chapter 8, verses 38 to 39.)